Florence Nightingale

Dorothy Turner

Illustrations by Richard Hook

Great Lives

William Shakespeare
Queen Elizabeth II
Anne Frank
Martin Luther King
Helen Keller
Ferdinand Magellan
Mother Teresa
Louis Braille
John Lennon
John F. Kennedy
Florence Nightingale
Elvis Presley
Captain Cook
Gandhi
Napoleon
Albert Einstein

First published in 1986 by
Wayland (Publishers) Limited
61 Western Road, Hove
East Sussex BN3 1JD, England

© Copyright 1986 Wayland (Publishers) Ltd

British Library Cataloguing in Publication Data
Turner, Dorothy
  Florence Nightingale. – (Great Lives)
  1. Nightingale, Florence – Juvenile literature
  2. Nurses – England – Biography – Juvenile
  I. Title   II. Hook, Richard   III. Series
  610.73′092′4   RT37.N5

  ISBN 0–85078–858–7

Phototypeset by Kalligraphics Ltd, Redhill, Surrey
Printed and bound in Italy by G. Canale & C.S.p.A., Turin

Contents

The Lady with the Lamp

At the height of her fame, during the Crimean War of 1854–6, Florence Nightingale became known as The Lady with the Lamp. The image of a saintly nurse carrying a lantern and walking among the poor wounded soldiers in a Turkish hospital, became forever associated with her name. It was an image the sentimental Victorians loved, but it gives a false picture of the real Florence Nightingale.

She did carry a lantern, and she did walk through the hospital at Scutari in Turkey every evening, comforting the sick and dying soldiers. She did indeed seem a saint to them. But, behind the popular romantic image she was a tough, clever, stubborn and brave woman.

Her time in the Crimean hospitals lasted less than two years. Her greatest work came later, during the last fifty years of her long life. After the Crimean War she retired from public view, but continued to work endlessly, sometimes frantically. Her achievements were enormous.

As a result of her work, hospitals ceased to be places of squalor, and nursing became the honourable, caring profession that we know today. Through her influence, the suffering of thousands of poor and sick people was eased, from the ordinary British soldiers to the wretched inmates of workhouses and the poorest peasants in India. She greatly raised the status of all women by the example of her own life's achievements.

Florence Nightingale was not just the Lady with the Lamp. She was someone much more remarkable.

Early days

Florence's parents, William and Fanny Nightingale, were married in 1818.

It was fashionable in those days for wealthy people to go on long tours of Europe, so accordingly, the newly-married couple left England at once and set off for the Continent, taking their servants with them. The Nightingales stayed abroad for three years, during which time Fanny gave birth to two daughters. The first they called Parthenope. The second, born in 1820, they called Florence, after the beautiful Italian city in which she was born.

When Florence was a year old her family returned to England. As they grew up, the girls spent their summers at the family's large country house in

Florence was named after the beautiful Italian city where she was born.

Florence and her sister Parthenope enjoyed a happy and privileged childhood.

Derbyshire and the rest of the year in their houses near the New Forest and in London. It was a busy life, as they had many cousins to play with and endless family gatherings to attend.

Until Florence was twelve she and her sister were taught by governesses. Their father then took over their education. He taught them classical and modern languages, as well as history, and mathematics, a subject which Florence always loved. It was a far better education than most girls received in those days.

Florence was clever and attractive but she was often unhappy. Sometimes her busy life seemed empty and meaningless. She saw the poverty of many people, living in poor homes, in sickness and misery, and even as a young child she always wanted to look after the sick, whether they were wounded dogs or broken dolls.

A call to serve God

When she was sixteen, Florence heard a call from God. She wrote in her diary: 'God spoke and called me to His service.' But what did He want her to do? Florence did not yet know.

In the meantime she continued to lead the life expected of her. She travelled abroad with her family, visiting museums and galleries, attending dances, concerts and dinner parties. She soon had many male admirers, which pleased her mother. Like all girls of her background, she was expected to make a good marriage.

In 1842 Richard Monckton

Florence wrote in her diary, 'God spoke and called me to His service.'

Milnes met the twenty-two-year-old Florence and fell in love with her. He was the ideal partner, and he wanted to marry Florence.

In those days women had little freedom of choice. There was no question of a woman choosing to have both a husband and a career. If she married, she would devote herself not to her own life, but to that of her husband.

Whether or not to marry Richard was an agonizing decision for Florence, and she made him wait seven years for her answer. Eventually she said no, she would not marry him. She had her own work to do. To give up the chance to lead her own life would, she wrote, 'seem like suicide'.

Her family were dismayed and angry at her decision and Florence almost collapsed under the strain of their opposition. But she heard God's voice again and shortly afterwards, on her birthday, she wrote: 'Today I am thirty . . . Now no more childish things. No more love. No more marriage. Now Lord let me think only of Thy Will . . .'

Florence's family were angry and dismayed at her decision not to marry.

The third path

'I had three paths among which to choose,' Florence reflected. 'I might have been a literary woman, or a married woman, or a hospital sister.' It was the third path that she wished to take. Yet the very idea of their daughter working in a hospital horrified her parents. They completely forbade her to do so.

It is not difficult to see why they opposed her plans. In those days hospitals were unbelievably squalid places, overcrowded and disease-ridden. Only the poor went to them and there they usually died.

Patients were packed together into huge, evil-smelling wards, where the walls were frequently splattered with blood and filth. Antiseptics to prevent infection were unknown. Surgeons, wearing coats caked in blood, cut off limbs with dirty knives and without any pain-killing drugs.

Nurses were untrained and

In Florence's time, nursing was not the respectable profession that it is today.

ignorant. Some slept in the patients' beds; others slept in wooden cages outside the wards. Most of the nurses were outcasts from society, having given birth to illegitimate babies. It is hardly surprising that many nurses became drunkards; no doubt alcohol helped to make their harsh lives more bearable.

No wonder, either, that Fanny Nightingale was appalled at the thought of her well-brought-up daughter working in these conditions. 'It was,' said Florence, 'as if I had wanted to be a kitchen-maid.'

11

Three months of joy

Florence arriving as a trainee at The Institute of Deaconesses, in Germany.

Florence had rejected marriage, but still she was not free to lead the life she chose. Now she became convinced that God had found her unworthy. It was a time of despair. She wrote in her diary 'I see nothing desirable but death ... why, oh my God, can I not be satisfied with the life that satisfies so many people?... My God, what am I to do?'

There was only one thing to do: she must take her life into her own hands. Bravely, she decided to spend three months learning about nursing at a training school at Kaiserwerth, in Germany. There were terrible family rows about her decision but Florence insisted on going.

It was scarcely the sort of place to attract anyone less dedicated than Florence. The Institute of Deaconesses, as the school was called, was organized on strict religious lines. Trainees rose at five in the morning, worked until seven at night and then began Bible study. The food was poor and the nursing training mediocre, but it was better than anything available in England.

Here Florence at last found something to stimulate her active mind. 'Now I know what it is to live and to love life,' she wrote at that time. But the joy was short-lived. After only three months she had to return to her family in London. Her mother and sister could hardly bring themselves to speak to her.

The Institute was run strictly. The training was mediocre and the food poor.

A nurse at last

Florence returned to live with her family. Much of the following year she spent nursing sick relatives – her father, her sister, a great-aunt and then her dying grandmother. It was not until 1853 that a friend suggested she should take on the job of superintendent at the Institute for the Care of Sick Gentlewomen, in London. Her mother and sister were aghast at the idea.

But Florence took the job. There was no salary, so her father made her an allowance of £500 a year, which was enough for her to live on. At last, it seems, he had decided there was no point fighting the wishes of his favourite daughter. Now she was free to be a nurse. She was just thirty-three years old.

Florence worked unpaid when she first started nursing in London.

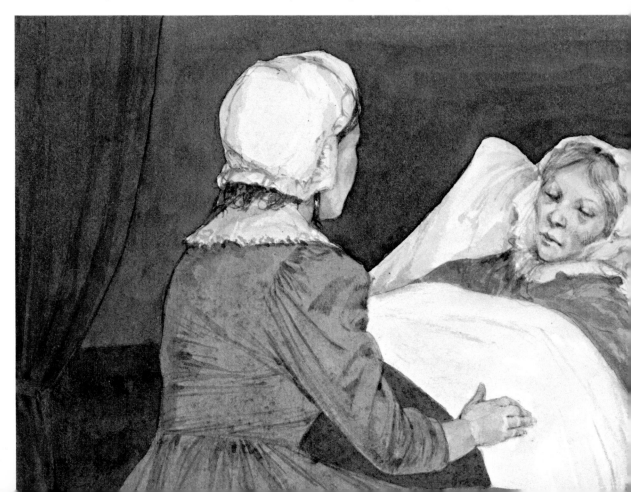

Florence ran the home for sick gentlewomen with astounding thoroughness. She organized a new hot water system, introduced a new kind of bell so that patients could call the nurses more easily, and had a simple form of lift fitted so that food could be hauled up to the wards from the kitchen. She had chair covers made, organized jam making to save money and chose the staff herself.

But it was hard to find good nurses. Often Florence did much of the work herself. She even went round the wards rubbing patients' feet to keep them warm!

Florence loved the hard work, as she had done in Germany. 'I am now in the heyday of my power,' she wrote. But she was about to be offered a greater challenge than she could have imagined. Within two years she was to become a national heroine. Soon everyone in England would know the name of Florence Nightingale.

The Crimean War

In 1854, Turkey, France and Britain declared war on Russia. British troops were sent to the Crimean peninsula, on the Black Sea, to attack the Russians. The battles that followed were violent and bloody, with heavy casualties. To make matters far worse, however, many men caught deadly diseases such as typhus and cholera. But the British army was so badly organized and poorly equipped that there were almost no medical supplies to deal with the sick and wounded.

William Howard Russell, a correspondent for *The Times,* sent back vivid reports from the Crimea, describing the terrible suffering of the soldiers. The people of Britain were outraged when they learned the truth, and there was a call for immediate action.

Sidney Herbert, then Secretary of State for War, had known Florence for some years and he admired her qualities greatly. Now he asked her to take a group of nurses to Scutari, in Turkey, to work in a hospital where British soldiers could be treated. Florence eagerly offered her services. Quickly she gathered a group of thirty-eight women, many of them nuns.

When they reached Turkey they found the situation to be quite desperate. At Scutari the army barracks had been turned into an emergency hospital. It was a huge gloomy building, containing no medical equipment and no furniture. Even worse, it was filthy, very damp, and stinking from the open sewers that ran beneath it. There was nothing to cook with, and very little water.

This terrible place was where Florence and her nurses were supposed to work. And all the time hundreds of wounded and sick men, many of them starving, frost-bitten and half naked, were arriving by boat from the Crimean Peninsula across the Black Sea.

Florence and her band of nurses arrive at the army barracks in Scutari to set up an emergency hospital.

The challenge of Scutari

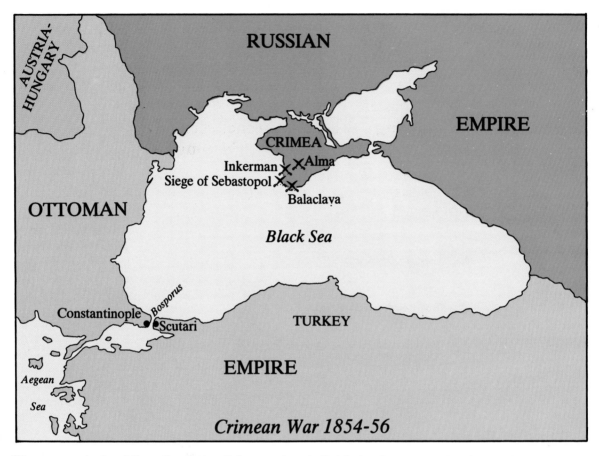

The wounded soldiers from the Crimean battlefields had to cross the Black Sea to reach the hospital at Scutari.

Florence, however, was not daunted. At once she set out to equip and organize the hospital. Fortunately she had brought some stores with her. Now she managed, somehow, to obtain many of the things they lacked, from sheets and medicines to socks and toothbrushes. She had the filthy wards cleaned and painted. She hired a house and set it up as a laundry where bedding could be washed. Then she reorganized the kitchens.

Some of the army doctors resented women interfering in

18

their work. They thought Florence was a nuisance, and she was certainly formidable. But, speaking always in her quiet and determined manner, she usually managed to get her own way.

She worked endlessly, compiling reports, suggesting improvements, organizing stores, even writing letters for soldiers unable to write themselves. Each night she walked the 6 km (nearly 4 miles) of corridors, carrying her lantern, visiting the sick and wounded packed together on the floor. She would speak to them and try to make them comfortable. Or, as happened so often, she would sit with a soldier while he died. In this place of cruel suffering, Florence seemed like a saint. Even the roughest soldier would not swear in her presence, and some men actually kissed her shadow as she passed.

Florence writes a letter home for a wounded soldier.

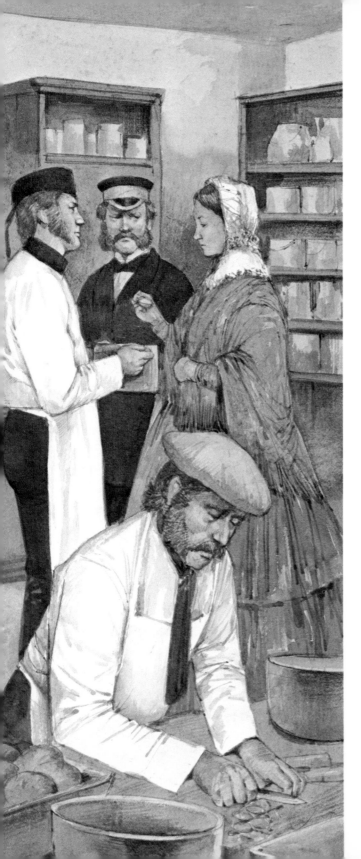

A national heroine

All this work took its toll on Florence's health. In May 1855, she was taken dangerously ill with fever. The doctors thought she would die, but at last she began to recover sufficiently to return to work.

By now the conditions at Scutari had been much improved. But Florence wanted to do more. She vowed to improve the lives of the soldiers, her 'children', as she called them. She brought in a French chef who introduced more appetizing and nourishing foods to replace broth made from boiled bones. She set up reading and writing rooms for the men, and arranged for teachers, books, games and writing materials to be sent out from England. She even collected the men's savings and sent them home to their families. Some of the older army officials thought she was 'spoiling the brutes'.

Back in England, the Lady with the Lamp was a national

Florence made many changes at Scutari. In the kitchens, she introduced nutritious foods to make sure that the soldiers were adequately nourished.

heroine, adored by the people. Donations poured into the Nightingale Fund that was set up to assist her work. Queen Victoria sent her a gold and diamond brooch inscribed with the works 'Blessed are the merciful'.

But there were still great problems, both at Scutari and at the hospitals in the Crimea. Cholera broke out again and many people died. However, at

The brooch Victoria gave to Florence.

The Queen admired Florence's hard work.

last the war came to an end.

In July 1856, Florence returned to England. Brass bands and welcoming committees waited to greet her, but Florence wanted nothing to do with all the fuss. So, travelling under the name of Miss Smith, she slipped unnoticed into London. There she caught a train for Derbyshire, walked to her home and arrived unannounced and alone, to her family's astonishment.

21

A political life

Florence arrived home pale, thin and exhausted. Yet once more she threw herself into work.

She never forgot her 'children', the British soldiers. 'I am a bad mother to come home and leave you in your Crimean graves,' she wrote. Thousands of these men had died from preventable disease, not from war wounds. Now she vowed to reform the army medical service so that the calamity of the Crimean War should not be repeated. To do this she would have to become a politician, but at that time there was no chance of a woman entering politics. So she worked

Sidney Herbert.

behind the scenes, expertly playing off one influential person against another and trying to persuade, or bully, politicians to take up her cause.

Florence had several meetings with Queen Victoria and the two women got on splendidly. 'We are much pleased with her,' wrote the Queen. 'I wish we had her at the War Office.'

As a result of Florence's efforts, a Royal Commission was set up in 1857 to examine the army medical service. Sidney Herbert, who had sent her to Scutari, was its chairman. Other members were Florence's allies from her Crimean days. She herself did much of the work. She inspected barracks and army hospitals, drew up charts, collected statistics, and compiled a 1,000-page document, in which she stressed the importance of good hygiene and a balanced diet in *preventing* disease. In those days this was quite a new idea.

Reform did come, but slowly. The first army medical school was founded, and conditions began to improve in army barracks throughout the country.

Right *Florence meets Victoria.*

'Poor Florence! Poor Florence!'

Florence spent much of her later life as an invalid, confined to bed, with many cats to keep her company.

Sidney Herbert, Florence's greatest admirer and ally, had worked long and hard with her on army reform. Then, in 1861, he became ill and died. His last words were reported to be: 'Poor Florence! Poor Florence! Our joint work unfinished'. Florence was shattered by his death. 'My work, the object of my life, the means to it, all in one, depart,' she wrote. But she herself had hastened Sidney Herbert's early death by persuading him to go on working despite his serious illness.

For months after his death Florence too was seriously ill. She locked herself away, and refused to see almost all visitors. For the rest of her life she was to remain an invalid, spending much of her time lying on a bed with her pet cats around her. Often she had to be carried from room to room.

But she continued to work, harder than ever. Incredibly, despite her weakness and ill health, she lived for another fifty years. Most of her greatest achievements were yet to come.

The Nightingale Nurses

During the remaining half century of her life, Florence worked on countless projects to help the sick and poor.

First she turned her attention to the general state of hospitals in England. Many of the existing buildings were woefully inadequate and unhealthy. So she wrote a book about hospital design. It was full of statistical tables, charts and diagrams and suggested ways in which hospital design could be improved. The Nightingale Training School was set up in the newly-built St Thomas' hospital in London. The trainees (called Nightingale Nurses) were given rooms in a wing of the hospital and received a thorough medical education. The School was such a success that other nursing schools sprang up around the country.

She also wrote a book on nursing, stressing the need for cleanliness, order, and 'consideration of the patient's feelings'. 'To be a good nurse,' she wrote, 'one must be a good woman.' This was a long way from the drunken outcasts who had staffed hospitals in the past. From her pioneering work grew the whole of our modern nursing profession.

The Nightingale Nurses.

The final years

At this time India was part of the British Empire. Although she scarcely ever went out of her house, let alone to India itself, Florence Nightingale did a great deal to lessen the suffering of both the British soldiers in India and the poorest Indian people themselves.

Florence managed to get another Royal Commission set up, this time to study medical conditions in India. Florence did much of the work behind the scenes. She wrote to every medical officer in India, gathering information. The Commission's report filled 2,000 pages of small print and revealed an appalling situation of poor diet, bad drainage and lack of basic hygiene. It was the beginning of a slow process of reform.

From her bed, Florence continued to offer advice, collect statistics, study, and write hundreds of letters. By her efforts the plight of the most desperately poor in England – the paupers in the workhouse hospitals – was eased. She undertook a three-year study of the health of mothers and newborn children. She also found time to write an enormous volume setting out her thoughts on religion and philosophy. And she always took an active interest in the progress of the Nightingale Nurses.

Florence took a great interest in the plight of the poor in England.

During these years Florence was almost always ill. Sometimes she felt that everything she had done had been a failure.

However, she continued working until her late seventies. Then, as her sight failed, she withdrew increasingly from the outside world. It was a lonely existence, for she outlived her family and her closest friends. The general public almost forgot that she was still alive.

In 1907 Florence, now very frail, was awarded the Order of Merit, an honour never before bestowed upon a woman. The award was delivered to her London home, but she hardly knew what she was receiving, merely murmuring 'Too kind, too kind.'

Three years later Florence died peacefully in her sleep, aged ninety. She had always hated the fuss of being a celebrity – what she called 'the fuzbuz about my name'. At her own request she was buried in the quietest style at a village church near her family's New Forest home. The words on her memorial stone read simply 'FN Born 1820. Died 1910.'

Florence was the first woman to be awarded the Order of Merit.

'So like a saint'

Florence and her nurses at St Thomas' Hospital, London.

Florence Nightingale gave her long life to serving God, who she believed was telling her to help fight poverty and disease. She did not achieve everything she set out to do, but the effects of her work can certainly still be seen today.

She changed the way people looked at the world. The status of nurses, soldiers, working women, were all viewed more favourably because of her example. She alerted people to the areas of society that many people preferred to ignore. And, bravely, she set about reforming them herself. Our clean and pleasant modern hospitals with their caring trained nurses grew from her pioneering work.

Many Victorians liked to think of Florence as a saint. Elizabeth Gaskell, a novelist who knew and admired her, described her unselfishness in caring for others. 'She is,' wrote Mrs Gaskell, 'so like a saint.'

But she also had a stubborn streak, as Mrs Gaskell recognized: 'She is so excessively soft and gentle in voice, manner, and movement that one never feels the *unbendableness* of her character when one is near her. Her powers are astonishing . . .'

Certainly Florence Nightingale could be difficult. She was always determined, sometimes unfair and ruthless. But how else could she have fought against her family's opposition, against society's narrow view of what women should be, against her own strong emotions, against powerful political opponents? How else could she have achieved so much in the battle to relieve human suffering?

Nurses today owe much to Florence's pioneering work.

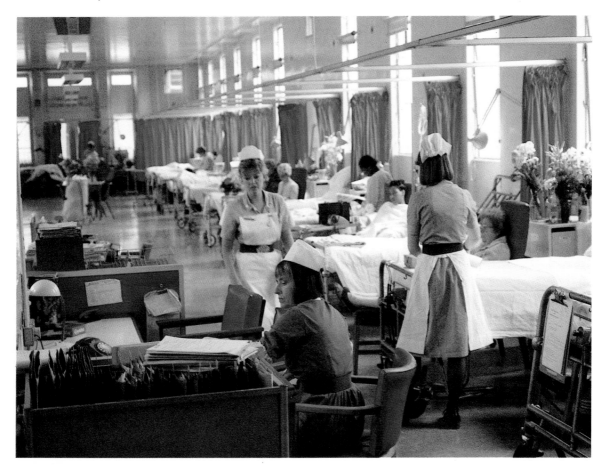

Important dates

1820 (May 12) Florence Nightingale born in Florence, Italy.

1837 She is called by God to do His work, but is not yet sure what this is to be.

1850 She decides not to marry, but to dedicate herself to God's work.

1851 Attends the Institute of Deaconesses at Kaiserswerth, Germany.

1853 Becomes Superintendent of an Institution for the Care of Sick Gentlewomen, in London.

1854 The Crimean War breaks out. Florence goes to Turkey, to work at the army hospital at Scutari.

1855 She is taken seriously ill with fever.
The Nightingale Fund set up to assist her work.

1856 Returns home to England, a national heroine.

1857 Royal Commission set up to study the army medical service.

1859 *Notes on Hospitals* published, explaining her ideas on hospital design.
Notes on Nursing published, setting out detailed guidelines on nursing.
Royal Commission set up to study medical services in India.

1860 The Nightingale Training School for nurses opened in London.

1861 Death of Sidney Herbert. Florence becomes an invalid. For the next 40 years she continues to work from her bed, seeing visitors only by appointment.

1865 Moves into her own house in London, bought for her by her father.

1874 Death of Florence's father.

1880 Death of Florence's mother.

1890 Death of Parthenope, Florence's sister.

1901 Forced to give up work because of failing eyesight.

1907 The Order of Merit conferred on her.

1910 (August 13) Death of Florence Nightingale.

Glossary

Anaesthetics   Pain-killing drugs, used to make patients unconscious during operations.

Antiseptics   Chemicals that kill bacteria and stop the spread of infection.

Cholera   A highly-infectious, usually fatal illness.

Hygiene   Cleanliness; the science of keeping people healthy.

Illegitimate   Born of parents who were not married to each other at the time of birth.

Order of Merit   A high honour bestowed on important citizens by the British monarch.

Nutritious Food   Provides good nourishment to keep the body healthy and strong.

Pauper A person who is very poor.

Peninsula   A strip of mainland projecting out into the sea.

Pioneering   Developing or starting something new.

Reformer   Someone who works to improve social conditions.

Royal Commission   A group of people chosen to study and report on a major problem or situation.

Statistics   Facts and figures.

Typhus   An infectious disease associated with poor living conditions.

Workhouses   Buildings where the very poorest people were sent to live and work in Victorian times.

Books to read

Florence Nightingale by Elspeth Huxley (Weidenfeld and Nicolson, 1975)

Florence Nightingale by Philippa Stewart (Wayland Publishers, 1973)

'Florence Nightingale' an essay in *Eminent Victorians* by Lytton Strachey (first published in 1918)

Florence Nightingale by L. du Garde Peach (Ladybird, 1959)

Lady in Chief by C. Woodham-Smith (Methuen, 1956)

Picture credits

Mary Evans Picture Library *title page*, 6, 8, 21, (top), 22; The Mansell Collection 11 (top); Topham Picture Library 13, 21 (bottom), 28, 29; Map on page 18 by Malcolm Walker. Cover artwork by Richard Hook.

Index